Into the Dark

Poetry by Caroline Ashe ~

this feels like a suicide mission - 2014

Poetry by Jonah Gabriel ~

Without Company - 2007

Thin Line - 2009

Caroline - 2013

Denae Publishing

Caroline Ashe & Jonah Gabriel

Into the Dark

Selected poems

Copyright © 2016 Caroline Ashe
Copyright © 2016 Jonah Gabriel

Denae Publishing 2016 (ISBN: 978-0-692-79190-5)

All rights reserved. This book or any portion thereof may not be reproduced or used in any manner whatsoever without the express written permission of the publisher except for the use of brief quotations in a book review or scholarly journal.

Cover design: Elaine Ward

Type is Times New Roman

Printed in the United States of America

Jonah Gabriel on Instagram ~@writeronstrike
Jonah Gabriel on Facebook ~ JonahGabrielpoet

In Memoriam

Jordan Denae Snider
1992 – 2011

You are missed,
you are loved,
always

Contents

is it identity theft if your shadow takes over?	1
there is no escaping reality	3
brain activity dwindling	5
migraines/association	6
abandon	8
shotgun	10
endure	13
crazy has witnessed a separation sickness	15
Thirty-Seven's A Long Way Away	17
fast fast, slow	19
in decision	21
slam	22
anger smiles	24
purge	25
cheer up and fall down	28
child's play	29
carry claustrophobia	30
suicide silence: :medicated mileage	32
throw the dice and slice it twice	34
responding to :: yours truly	35
sleeping	37
i count nine stars	39
death clock ticking	41
polaroid camera	43
quick fix and new tricks	45
somehow everyone is sleeping but i'm still wide awake	47
extermination	48
stereo steps	50
her letdown	51
sugarcoating insecurity	52
sharp objects	53
unprotected	55
no poise, just poison	57
clarity	58
fingers, carrots, and demerits	59
taste of medication in the mourning	61
submachine dirty pop	62

Contents continued...

inspiration was only a thought of you away	65
the last nail	67
sub pop machine	69
grief	71
under God / Into the Dark	72
state of balance	74
crossfire	76
18	79
the possession	81
the incident	83
untitled	85
rising son	86
daisies	87
conversation	89
blinding	90
atmospheres	93
April	94
blending	95
distortion	96
the long road	98
thank you page	103

Into the Dark

is it identity theft if your shadow takes over?

i lost my identity on Middlewood lane
i barely knew my name
walking around, hiding the pain
i lost my identity on Middlewood lane

some reason i couldn't understand
your name etched into my being
couldn't stop the beating
my heart couldn't stop the craving

sketched out a little
love, didn't want to hear another goodbye
i kissed you goodnight
another time

never thought it'd come back
attempting a new portrait
painting a new pretty,
still don't feel like it's enough
i lost my bravery
in someone else's concerned words

can't help but look at you
but still i am
worrying, loving
worrying, giving up
can't find the truth
but it feels so real when i'm with you

what to trust
the doubt, the dream
the love, the lust
it's all about
where i choose to be
here alone,
or at home again

in your arms

don't know the street name
but i felt found,
playing hide and seek
with the sound of
mesmerized moments

should i let go
all the inhibitions keeping me from you
or unlock your fingers from mine
and release myself from
the idea that
perfection was a call away

charlatan beauty
a calming voice
forgotten in a time capsule
not pretty enough
to be seen differently
than the dirt i live in

can't forget all the smooth
charming things you said
can't decide if all the things were meant
or if i'm just another fool getting lied to
just like you
why do i feel like
i'm just like you

call me Caroline, call me Ashe
call me Caroline, call me Crashe
this is who i am, changed from trash
to a better girl in a flash
i find my identity in the words and the gashes
another poem and i'm past this

call me Caroline, call me Ashe
or better yet...don't call me at all

there is no escaping reality

sheets of calloused light,
like a solar eclipse
cross over, closed
unable to clothe me completely
in anything other than a warmer cold

i wished once for you to help me
endure it, delude me into thinking
unbalanced crises make
remorseful folks
instead of criminal fools
captioned in newspapers as
gruesome accidents

but you were too bold
striking cowardice and practice in the same sentence
believing genius is shame
coated in cinnamon faith

hostility began to brew
and my independency of you grew
i could see through,
through your borderline blinders
benign as they had seemed

they finally were deemed
a banal cry out to the slaved man,
to chain him to your post
and create your own world
with him crushing competing plans
reminding him of his place as ghost

my dearest Luna had to hide
as Helios was beguiled
your charm worked its magic
and Helios no more was a halo,

though he sang praise
very pure and moving
giving a false feeling of
safety

but there is no safety
in your words, no matter who sings them
only lies and destruction
the demise and creation of
the line between good and bad

and Helios reached out,
with only sweet words to guide me back,
he said he could fix, that he could help me endure,
and frequenting naive trust
i was burned

fixating, after
instilling tanked stimulants
and heaven-reaching depressants
i found that there is an understandably deteriorating universe
governed by the will of Aero and his seven sons
and that there is no middle ground now,
incapacitated in a pool of indiscretion, too vivid
the darkness, too lyrical the light

no matter what
there is no escaping reality

brain activity dwindling

nine o'clock and waiting for
the day's end
but i'm beginning to notice

the day never ends
just runs into the next
until eyesight becomes hazy
and even learning
and acknowledging my identity
is useless

commercial after commercial
advertising things that could
go right in my existence
but they last only half a minute
and then the reruns begin
againagainagain

i search, wondering
if there's a point to
the incessant headache
of my life

and i realize
where i once had direction, aspiration
now lies "Wrong Way" signs on every corner

and i realize
the self-discovery prospect
isn't working

because matter how hard i try
i can never discover
where they've hidden
the lost and found

migraines/association

but the words don't come
taking tomorrow by the neck
and choking it

..waiting for the ever after
i was promised, no longer is
forever beating against my chest

/but waiting
doesn't last forever
unless i choose

the drowning, the laughing
the coughing, the booze

thorns caressing skin
drinking needles
this is love again,

and the dream becomes a killer
interrupting quiet loves
a memory to hold onto

,here,
no existence

cruel jokes that
interpret actions backwards

a coma existing only for me to survive
nothing happens after
or before
waiting

and i feel it

waiting
;dying
it's breeding, killing me
and families

breaks in the sky
jump into a universe
where

i am creating fireworks
i am creating deadly quirks
the sadness it lurks

and the syringe deep into my skin,
is no longer
a breath of blind coincidences
and powerful liars

the syringe is a vaccine
keeping me safe, keeping me brave

it is keeping me right
next to you
in chains

burning out
it costs to watch the dying pass
onto the living once more

left behind
to undo you, undo me
my heart still climbs to save yours

the mountain is too high to climb this time...

abandon

turning the mess up louder
words i cannot claim,
but recognize deep within the core
endless frustration
car ride reminders
sitting drunk, calling yesterday back
screaming

--why did you leave
why did you take the
only chance i ever had
at forgetting--

locked doors,
keeping them out
or keeping me in
it's tomorrow i'm afraid of
restless, watching
shivers graze the skin

razors dig deeper
while i'm searching for reason
i am silent, hiding in cowardice
just a mime running into a brick wall
hoping someone will save me
but no one takes notice

no faith in tomorrow
no trust in today
i keep wishing for you to come back,
my dear yesterday

i feel the tears upon my cheeks
demanding me to acknowledge
all the things i ignore
i'm still not ready to say

"i can't pretend anymore"

so i just plead and plead for the tears
to stop- to dry,
unprepared to face
yesterday's disgrace
i close my eyes
and drown in words
staring down shadows
fooling myself into believing
they will protect me

abandoning healthy habits
letting the worst of me take over
thinking of when i didn't know
thinking of when i didn't see
forgive me, yesterday,
as i forget to breathe

yesterday you have left me
and i am lost
i will search for tomorrow
with razors digging in
finding solace in the clarity
of this abandonment

shotgun

she just

wants to remember how it feels
to be overwhelmed by anger,
wants to remember how to be mean,
how to scream,
how to make others bleed.

she just

keeps listening to angry men
that go nowhere
and wants to be just like them

they sing songs about hate,
how it can make or break a man
they sing songs about drunken plans,
killing time, memories that create
the demons that help them rhyme
and the women they hate,
they're so fucking irate

she just

keeps blaring them
deafening out the surrounding
dears, queers, and her stupid fears
so close to breaking
so close to taking
separating yesterday
from her tomorrow
only anger, never sorrow

and she's just me

but i'm not angry.

i'm not mean.
i don't know how to make others bleed.
i don't even know how to make them need.

i'm just

getting devoured by the feeling,
of a loneliness creeping.

i just

don't want to burn out here

i just

want to disappear

and all i can think of is you,
wish you were red, wish i wasn't blue
wish you could take me away
wish all this was through

you could just

save me from this house,
this emptiness, this town.
we'd leave all this behind
and find better lives;

go somewhere no one will find us.
where tomorrow is a blessing
not a thought we're second-guessing

holding hands
falling from airplanes
the rush of life on our faces
never assuming
tomorrow is easy
never confusing

sadness with normality

and the ones from our pasts,
they'd just

forget, continue on
with sadder lives and screaming knives.
after a while our memory would be
myth;
something no one could trust
except for the lust
of leaving it all
just like us.

she is just me

screaming inside
watching past present and future collide
listening to angry men believe.
remembering but no longer grieving
tracing old scars
wanting to run away to the stars
..............begging for clarity
..............begging for you to come with me

she just

screams

endure

in silence it grows, the pain
blisters under the skin
but it does not belong to me

it's burning like a match
marks and holes, we flicker
in and out, i
can't face the music, and
the lyrics can't be found

but your goodbye sings;
reverberating in my skull
the things you never said
the things you always...

disappeared, hands shaky
thoughts stunted
eyes out of focus

tends to get hazy,
though the sickness never gets lazy
it's not October but we're both blue
my hands, they're weak too
they're too, they're too small
i cannot catch you, so we'll both fall

trying to hide the noose,
all i seem to do
is tighten the knot

passing cars, strangers
make eye contact, but no connections
both of us with a pale complexion,
we don't share affections

though maybe we share

a choked inflection -a hidden infection-
cold eyes and a broken heart
laughing out of fear
it's because of you that i'm here

in body and mind,
it's you that you can't find
in company, and alone
alone, and in company

festering views like maggots -tragic-
leaving and now you're no longer breathing,
unconsciously, this is just you
breeding inside me, the poison it spews
you can't just stop

you won't reach the bottom
you won't reach the top
stuck in limbo
there's nowhere to go...

the sky is too big,
the stars are too many
to find you this time
i will not follow,

but though this journey through my mind
and the hopes of you alive
is pulling me apart
i am running

from -towards-
you

crazy has witnessed a separation sickness

in my bones, screeching sounds that let me know
the race was lost, my evenings tossed,
crazy's here to pick me up, throw me around
my only date, but it's too late
gagging me, i don't make a sound

bottle drinking my mind it's sinking
keep seeing you, though i know you're gone
dead phone still calls,
i just wonder if you remember at all
it's almost dawn and i can feel the pain
but it's all the same it's all the same

it wasn't my fault; ask the damned violin
playing tunes that bring me to ruins
before we touched, i never knew sin
i swear, i swear, it's not again (again)
crazy just loves me, but i can leave again

bottle drinking my mind it's sinking
keep seeing you, though i know you're gone
dead phone still calls,
i just wonder if you remember at all
do you remember at all?

a grin taped to my face
an aching of glass bottles breaking
caked to my sides, symptoms of demise
it tastes like mold, death gets so old
but blood comes seeping, and i'm almost surprised
it's just another prize, another

bottle drinking my mind it's sinking
keep seeing you, though i know you're gone
dead phone still calls,
i just wonder if you remember at all

it's almost dawn and i can feel the pain
but it's all the same
it's all the same

envelope kissed, only one love left to send
running from my end
the distance from reality takes its toll
tripping on laces, braced for my mortality;
i'm not whole
but it's alright, i still have a good mentality
with, without reality

bottle drinking my mind it's sinking
keep seeing you, though i know you're gone
dead phone still calls,
i just wonder if you remember at all
it's almost dawn and i can feel the pain
but it's all the same it's all the same

just wish you were by my side
cuz then i could begin to fight
i'm losing i'm losing it tonight
contagious, the sickness in my mind
i'm losing, i'm losing the fight

Thirty-Seven's A Long Way Away

and the pieces fell down,
all the pills swallowed never made a sound
year after fucking year
wasted on me,
i forgot what it was like to feel eternity
breathing down your neck

fucking break down the walls
if you turn and see, there's nothing left at all
i hear the words that entered me
the ocean's tide splashing across the sea
(she never moved on, no she never moved on)

just walked away, counted lies
broke all the ties
it was her last free breath
she knew she wished she had never left
but it's too late to see
that the polls we've taken all agree
that she's so broken hearted,
just gone crazy
that she's, that she's still me

fucking break down the walls
if you turn and see, there's nothing left at all
i hear the words that entered me
the ocean's tide splashing across the sea
(she never moved on, no she never moved on)

shock me, shock me
(come on, shock me baby)
treat me with a smile
tell me it'll be okay
that it's all worthwhile
but don't forget to lace
each syllable you say

with the bitter taste of acid
with the acrid smell of bile

fucking break down the walls
if you turn and see, there's nothing left at all
i hear the words that entered me
the ocean's tide splashing across the sea
(she never moved on, no she never moved on)

she's hiding in the corner
the corner inside me,
she just keeps repeating
there's no one home tonight
no, there's no one home tonight (no one home tonight)

another pill reaching, deeper inside me
searching for the reason
for what's eating away at my sanity
but the pill's just breaking me
it's making me remember
it's making me see
the beauty of eternity
when there's no one home,
no one home tonight to see

no i never moved on,
no i never,
never moved on

fast fast, slow

sky light,
dreaming, darken/lightening
Lightning
sharp bursts of beautiful
wake me up, tell me
i love you,
when you wake me up
and i can see forever

shadows
picturing brightly, softly
seeing through the back
the heart is beating
stars above are singing,
rock star Punched screaming
fast paced slow

breathing in the scent of
understanding
the dark can't catch me today;
so fast, i'm running; but i'm not
running away

straight towards you- darkness
scared yet, to turn away?
straight towards you, baby
opening closed doors seems so easy
when my eyes are smiling this way

loose,
won't lose
bruises showing i have
chosen darker roads
tonight let's take it easy
and make the prettiest mess

you can have me.
it's so much better when

i'm free
sick of being, lonely
sick of watching life go on;
take it in my hands
and Squeeze

terrifying/
amplifying
it's just a little catch,
don't know how long this one will last;

three four five a.m.
time for more
the sky opened up
and told me,

this is the way it's supposed to be.

in decision

back up
panic don't go manic
running around the world
moving only in circles around my house
thinking maybe sometime soon,
it'll bring me somewhere new

Peter lays beside me-
a toy i was given for my choice of indecision
hate and love
so close and yet so far
i don't recognize me anymore

i regret to inform you that time has not changed me
this is only going to last so long
listen to Terri
only the mask can save me-
and i am so tired of hiding from reality

up and down
time to visit crazy town
no more cuts, no more bruises
but physical pain has so many uses

it's time to choose
do i want to win or do i want to lose?
time's up-
i lose

slam

shriek
to the ceiling cracks and the heavens dive into
my half empty cup of water and cleaner
it never tastes so sweet until the last breath smiles up at you
bleed in the poison
syringe the insane right
into out of forever with but always without

fuck
to the sound of my tears
violence and vehemence
so scared i try to breathe in oxygen
maybe too much maybe too less
and stated by the loves own lie
you have no home
you have no life
surrounded by void the lust-less time

dream
to the bashing of walls
hiding closets give me a casket
don't open keep closed
hide me away don't lead me astray
dead in mind
voices cash in dollars and nickels
wasting the once blinding sunshine into
even lightning bugs are more vibrant to say
i hate you i'm the better part of you
i'm the perfect parasite
but i'll cringe in your sight
freedom in fright
delusion in a solo fight

dance
to the grievances of my
never tell a lie friends

all the promiscuous dead ends
rhyming to the beat
heart barely sings
too fast too slow
which way do they want me to go
a box of wishes that aren't met
a tennis match with my feelings that's still not set
it's a moment
the weighted monster that hates and bruises
a man in black a man in white
the scary invisible
the ugly that's visible

watch
to the breakdown dream
a bad ending scene
a tragedy
a little slice of me
insanity

anger smiles

swimming out to see the disaster in plaster
a new you every day
you're rock hard and so very vacant
not even a heart of ash resides inside your shell
i pity you

dreaming of chocolate cyanide
i drink my size in morphine
to let the kook within the kill, breathe again
life without is such a sin
i never would have begun my heinous crime
if it wasn't for you, my sweet lovely lie
whom made me think a thought of delight
that ended at the first sight of light

a dog of death at mXXy feet
leave the chair of relief
there's no reason to stay
until, me, Ms. Conflict, goes away
didn't you know
it all goes to hell

who screams reality
when all that looks stunning
is leaving
falling, running
who screams
when the wolf howls goodnight

it's crowded in my head
And it's beating musical notes of terror
and as the music plays
i sink into everything
i sink to hide
the quiver inside
i sink into forever

purge

pure
such an innocent drive
sloww at yellow stopp at red
gogogo at green
take a right

pure
air conditioner on
listening to that song
one time it meant so much
but by now it's just hit-or-miss
and tremolos timorous
but it's not so bad
another broken stoplight

pure
energy energy energy
nicotine kisses lips
friendly (and deadly) fries
backstab
lurch
an ambulance

pure
months without him
days without razors
minutes without knives
and seconds without tears
find whisper dr. and take a right

pure
gutters greet pretty
the street sparks dirty
windshield wipers squeak
gasoline cheap with expertise
still so innocent

take the highway

pure
salute the sleet
the homeless man on the street
throw out the burns and everything
which meant so much that means so less
the burned cd
radio rips replaces reappears
awkward smiles and horrid thoughts
make this the best
turn left ahead

pure
inside screech
shriek scream shrill
last seen on evergreen st.
and still
car by car by car
it's not too easy it's too easy
not to care what isn't really there

pure
such a corrupted drive
drive right through yellow
speed up at red
still gogogo at green
not stopping for anyone or anything
a stop sign a dead end
still straight ahead

pure
operation of innocence
i thought it all made sense
before
and now
open the trunk
is it day or is it night?
does it matter?

pretty little shiner
black and so beautiful
pull the trigger tainted
emotion emasculation

once pure now purge

cheer up and fall down

capsizing
deciding against
the obvious decision
that's the worst of the best
the beast within the beauty
forwarding spam
i am i am i am
never mind i can't remember
like an experimented rat that
wants the cheese
but never can remember colours
to bring salvation

capsizing
platter of decaying skittles
in front of me
i eat until i puke
needing graham crackers and cigarettes
i don't even smoke
i think i only need to choke
on the smoke of disabled decisiveness
like a fabled fantasy with prince charming to fix the bruises
not to use or abuse
that is the only answer that i can find

capsizing
flipping over senses
recovering from the stench of death
sticking to clothes like
duct tape to a broken heart-
it stays a while but ripples through the river
and becomes nonexistent
deteriorating immediately
so no one notices
they're missing me

child's play

going on home
with a fiery heart
adrenaline painted winter violet
wine on cream carpet
cars chasing
hide and seek tag or red rover?
red rover red rover
send the Chevy right over
speeding sixty
let it crush
my broken body baby

my head held heavy
let the road crack,
earth quake
mind at stake
it's a sanity attack
so let it rip open my soul
with
peaceful relief
and a puddle of dead memories
in the cupboard with all my mourning glories

jump the gun
shoot the cliff
run into wrists
slit the street
hear the beat
of everything
dying and flying
rewinding senses with only strangers
watching me
playing devil's advocate
with my life
red rover red rover
Chevy come run me over

carry claustrophobia

Saturday's cold companion
plays with my hair
whispers soft-spoken secrets
in ears red and frostbitten
leaving to
railroad tracks corrupted
here lie memories
stumbling downward
Saturday's sad shipmate
follows us down
walking
feet moving forward
nothing lies in front of or behind
ignite the fire that will never again exist
hopeless wishes
Saturday was every other day i missed
falling into rocks and wooden planks
falling into always ending English epigraphs
perhaps
the splinters in my hand
will bleed
envelope's last kiss
leave it in the mailbox
what a note
beating belligerently
songs swaying
playing
Saturday's midnight monster
drinking bottled beverages
ripping gashes into my heart
remember blank pages
useless stages open curtains
closed coffins
eyeliner easy
lovely lashes
carrying claustrophobia on my back

clenching my teeth to the heavy weight
waiting for
searching for
nothing
Saturday's apprehensive alliance
dying for rhetorical romances
rocking out to killer classical
releasing stress through breaking glass
another rapture another mask
Saturday's ponderous position
my last requisition
one hopeless mission
Saturday's last cold blast
and Sunday's first living hearse

suicide silence: :medicated mileage

driving on along the road at midnight
watching gas stations fly by
neon lights gasping for breath
the smell of cigarette smoke and lime hovering over

noticing my hands shaking and discoloured
i decide
to pull over to a parking lot
smokes on one side
a mattress on the other
which do i find more important?
sleep rest time to relax
raspy voice toxins time to relax

i choose toxins
coffee
and skittles
$7.40

and now to
close these wide eyes
lullaby surprise in disguise
thirty-six dollars a night
all i need is some lights out
some mindless show
static on the radio

typing half intelligible murmurings
onto my keyboard
remembering all the things that brought me here
all the things Forget would never forgive
things that not even missy mj
and doctor dee could carry away
on a copper platter

another drag

another drop
another handful
another endless thought

shining badges
cleaning guns
i'm the sheriff
it's only a bullet through my heart

all i have left is a static suicide
and a missing deputy

throw the dice and slice it twice

blade to wrist
blood to kitchen floor
trigger, so sinister
cocked and ready to party
let's dance around in emo town
traffic just getting started
noose too loose
lost in the cyanide cries
you lie through your teeth
just to get underneath my skin
you win
trigger, so sinister
let the blood flow
the water in the tub swimming to the tile
a waterfall of gas and fire, water and desire
disaster in plaster
skin churning and burning
me yearning for
a little more
vodka in the bottle
but it's dripping to the kitchen floor
creep and crawl slip and screech
drink the sink's worth in bleach
reach for more but i'm too weak
and i see, weary and bleary
the ever after is no more

responding to :: yours truly

it was with you
that my world fell through
destined to be faulty
pieces of a broken mirror
lay heavy reflecting only
my cornered and crushed heart

it was with you
that my world fell through
dark bags under green eyes carry
my smile
the beige bags
are turned upside-down
and everything inside them
falls

it was with you
that my world fell through
taking my words home
and throwing me out
i never should have given you
my days my nights
the beating of my heart

it was with you
that my world fell through
giving me words to say
i'd never hope to keep
but would never give away
-you're the reason i still
keep forever in my vocabulary

it was with you
that my world fell through
twisting and turning
watching knots form in my stomach

i hate to need
to know
to want something more
than what it is to be
alone

it was with you
that my world fell through
caring less than needed
i don't want you to see me
shocked, simply

sleeping

wake up
the sun is shitting on the world-
rays too ugly, bright, love to shine down and
glorified grandiose get-up-and-go workers
love to say good morning to
those with sallow bags under tired eyes
those who slit their wrists to smile up at the sun-
blinding

with hate for hopeless hell-risen light
i wish for a night time
that lasts
as long as i do

wake up
the leaves are wrestling
on branches- barely staying strong
waving to the breeze
sexing themselves up for
straight suicides
they fall fall
fall

i watch them to see
if i could ever be
half as strong
as what they used to be

wake up
the world is circumcising young atheists
in the shadows of extremist
youth groups and catholic churches
that hang little boys and girls for Jesus's profit
giving good great grey gruesome lectures to
save those going to the lowest levels of Hell

level seven is my best friend-
i will go down in history without
knowledge of where i went when i went to
who remembers me in a broken destiny
suicide notes and nothing stressed but
a single singer, a neck-ringer on the side

wake up
dead poets talk in the evening
conversing condemning concerning
suicide another try too many lies
holes in hearts
how are you supposed to bandage a broken heart?
the Band-Aid keeps falling off with each beat
beat beat of my heart
the dead poets reply with a scream

i only hear a whisper in the night
all alone rocking back and forth
back and forth
tears playing tag with my eyeliner
oh, no oh, no
there my brain goes,
off onto another fucking forgivably forgetting forever tangent-
who knows how to stop?

wake up
to
reality-
wake up
and
wake me too

i count nine stars

key words left typing, trying
they still haven't been said
as lies replace truth
and softly kiss my lips with cinnamon sugar in the mix
all i have are plastic wedding rings

i watch the tv
off like any faith i once had
i pretend that my dreams play on
i weave stories and scarves for you sweet darling
but i'll remember the strangle forever
all i have are rusty razors

how many glass pieces will mend my broken heart?
my yesterdays?
last words typing, withholding
all things crash down upon
sweet denying defying dying
too close to you
all i have are crumbling walls

listening to the hiss of steam
the seams of my mended heart cut
i just wish it meant something when
chance the romance of the vomit veracious
to the glass bowl contagious
wasted
all i have left is the flip of the coin

macaroni and cheese
mashed moments won't you please
kept in the pocket stall for a second
menthol wides beside
pink phone and a dial tone drink me dry
every door is closed but one
wine bottle in ruins

red paint insane but what's left to taint?
all i have left is a starfish and a hand-me-down wish

what is left in me, is there something you don't see?
not even when pigs fly (to the top the spinning top)
but envelopes can hold the hope you didn't take
mail it across the world
but maybe instead bottle it shake it up wait until it pops
then its opened and empty so just break
all i have left is a signature

blanket the windows it's a vampire store
scratches screeches ashes and leeches
pictures hide the walls with memories i'd care not to share
maybe i'll pretend that they were never there
lies still kiss but so much harder- chocolate mint
falling into the rabbit's hole i'm always letting go
hiding behind bangs it's the death star the death stare
i can't stay until morning tomorrow won't come here
useless now
all i have is

death clock ticking

soul-stealing-stew
i would never make it for you
throwing my paper heart at your neck
slicing ever so slightly
but enough to see you're bleeding
i enjoy your yelp with a grin

soul-stealing-stew
i would never make it for you
feeding you lies remaking his demise on video
seeing your sorrow as his skull is crushed in
i cruise along the highway
with your tears washing my car

soul-stealing-stew
i would never make it for you
my head-ache barely breathing
i wish to watch you sink so slowly
but in a blink i find you struggling under the sea
i can hear you screaming in my mind
Advil attacks you from behind

soul-stealing-stew
i would never make it for you
broken dreams breeding
we both seem to lead it to our memory
ever so slightly we try to fight it
but all that's left is ugly
we leave in a hurry holding hands
in my head he reprimands
everything you stand for
the yesterdays before

soul-stealing-stew
i will always make for you
three stars together leader leave here

start the car with lies
forget the horrid weather
pretend to remember the things you'll never know
whisper softly wanting
sleep in waiting doomsday repeating

soul-stealing-stew
i taste it, swallow it with ease
forever making drinking the disease
i'll last too long before long
it won't it will goodbye and descend
break and bend mend and condescend
breach the wall reach out and ready to fall
it'll bring me to the floor,
on my knees leaving letting go of my lost soul
always i'll be failing tainted and screaming
always i'll be
always i'll be empty

polaroid camera

old music tangos through the speakers
words that used to comfort me in fall
now just make me hurt for yesterday's forgotten miseries
and today's horrid halls

silent sincerity monitors all of the lies in the corner of my eye
and my soul is stolen, sealed up far away in fall's last cry
or at least it seems that way
judging by the midnight's cool breeze ;;
it tastes like the delicious mix of
chaos chocolate milk and razorblades

grand pianos fall to the floor in an
attempt to stop the pounding keys
the jolts through their bodies the seizure of their minds ;;
they crash into corruption
leaving me stirring ready for their resurrection

tulips kiss winter's funeral fruition
a waking of a withering time
my wavering admission
leaves traces of the sketch's line
in a polaroid camera
cleansed by waltzing snowflakes

memorization of the mimicking kind
let's rewind and play this all over
i don't want to watch you cry this time
as the wind whistles and seagulls fly

stars tisk tisk tisk their tongues in disapproval
we were both a little unusual
who says fall and winter don't mix
who says seagulls don't play tricks
who says grand pianos never say i love you

-a polaroid camera leaps into the sky
leaving lovely pianos lying seagulls
lost memories and seasons far behind

quick fix and new tricks

fearing those who are everything to her
imagining the nothing falling into her
she runs down the lane
walks through the flames
tries to tame the beast
that is eating away at her like a disease

go forth she cries
as the little dog laughs
leave now she screams
as the lonely shepherd dreams
she doesn't want them to see
the ugly side of everything she claims to be::

walking away from all she hopes to be::
ugly has always been her pretty
only fifteen, going on twenty
years pass, they never last
as life fades away into her black hair flies in the wind
takes a turn for the worst and she falls back into
her mind, sitting on an empty shelf,
let's re:: reality
sitting on an unkempt bed hoping for some mental health
instead of...

magical powers are her secret
oh, yes, you know she'll keep it
locked away in that golden cage
don't read her mind don't [try to] read her mind
it makes you feel dyslexic and too dramatic
close her book and leave it
keep the fairy tales locked away [in a wrought iron cage]

fearing those who are everything to her
imagining the nothing falling into her
she runs down the lane

walks through the flames
tries to tame the beast
that is eating away at her like a disease

this is a slice of what it's like to be
insanity.

somehow everyone is sleeping but i'm still wide awake

sleeping in a state of comatose
hoping something makes itself just a bit more clear
in a good way;; bringing good jolly cheers
things are always muddy murky misinterpreted in me

fall and fail and flail your arms trying not to drown
understand nothing is left now
crying makes nothing better
killing one bird with three stones,
too inebriated to throw straight
because of the hate
the sadness in that last letter

darling i'm dying in myself
and don't you remember that it's possible-
mental suicide? childlike in what i want to be
nothing like the real me

knives strewn across the floor
instead of wanting more;; all i want is less
less is more, you should know
less is more, just needs deeper deeper
cutting through to the bone
pain is still my vacation home

maul the truth, call it lies, my demise
every time i see you smile, a little life returns
but every time i see you cry
all i want to do is die

never ending story of pathetic;; i don't like me
or i don't see anything real, fake is all i feel
wait until the end is clear
hope until the end is near

shit fuck damn ;; kill me now.

extermination

beauty comes by
once in a while
i surrender to it

cuckoo cuckoo cuckoo
the clock mocks me
what time is it
what time is it
it's time
to back away from

over and over
same mistakes
i can't keep making
the same mistakes

burning
just burning
my blood burns a hole in my skin
but the smile burns a hole in my heart

all i see is killing me
it's the same thing
closing in
walls closing in,
my body is closing in
it limits me
walls attached
comforting to know
i'm killing me...
you're killing me

/from the inside
you and me
we just sit and watch
the moon

i already killed a part of me:
the part you loved
you were begging for forever
with my enemy
just another minute goes by
wasting my time
i'm begging for forever
without pain

filtered,
my skin leaks
so pretty pretty pretty
...i'm killing me

stereo steps

the last cigarette sleeps
in fingers dried from sheets
of wind cowering frost

the ash falls in dreams, eyes
meet once but never, she sings
pure as snow falling

falling

but angels grow wings and
she soars well out of reach

membrane coma rakes across
tear stained cheeks enveloping
air, the struggle to breathe, to be

it's roulette, as the stereo steps across
heartbeat, thump tha thump weakened,
the nightmares unapologetic remedy

the scars return, under stress and
frightening nerves, tweaked alcoholic
a systematic overload

but the snow is falling pure and slow
and the cigarette burns down upon
the dried fingers as the last of the ash falls

falls

and she has her wings soaring

just out of reach

her letdown

after the fireworks
she stands outside
wishing her dreams
were a reality
or maybe just a nearby memory
cherished as all gorgeous lies should be

another black out leaves her
crying - scared - lost in the demon's grasp
her heart beat skips like a scratched cd
who knows if she'll ever be the same

her knees shake
the world has gone missing
and there she stands-
lonely as static speaks by her in a room of white
so many people cloud her vision
panic attacks and claustrophobia
follow her like a loyal German shepherd

hungry for new adventures
who would guess that
it's mania at its best
who would guess that
she's ready to go
and she does-
like the end of a play
she takes a bow
and disappears

sugarcoating insecurity

candle wax breathing into me,
skin deep.
i wait for the epiphany,
the fire ignited deep inside me.
but none come and here i sit,
waiting for you to return my everything.

caramelized lies
resting on my tongue,
too sweet for me to swallow.
i let them linger,
trying to adapt,
to digest the possibility of
another kiss.
impossible.

burning candle,
speaking to me softly,
reaching into my soul;; searching.
do i listen?
frowning, challenges lay in front;;
behind, the way as it was.
which way to go?
as the wick flickers out.

the war inside,
the world outside-
alone, undermining me,
uncertainty flows.
a white rose bleeds
like a child sweating on a hot day,
ice cream dripping down his arm.
sticky situations
now bulimic from too much candy.

breeding hostility like rabbits,

chest tightens, image ripens,
if only you could see
the deeper side of me.
lighting the wick,
i can barely see.
please come find me.

candle burns;
yearning for sweet candy
i ask for more.

sharp objects

in the sheets
there is blood rising
flesh peddling
to a God
that i continue
praying
to

ashes on the floor
mixing toxicology

slumbered eyes
frostbitten in
oxygen's slow release

a Cross crucifying
slowed thought
and hands
clasped with
shadows dancing on
midnight's wall
joining of souls
eclipsing
the sharp objects
doing damage

weakened in
a pouring religion
circling halos
as R.E.M. sets
a slow motion capture
before the blood
runs out
and Jesus
turns deaf to
pleading

liquid rosary
slurs into dream
and hands become
melting flesh
into flesh
Hers and mine
joining before
the last conscious
wake
rises with the blood
in the sheets

unprotected

peak my interest
a poem just my size
afraid of power
but using it so well
it's incredible
finding the father
of charm
and taking him to dinner
The Casanova of all time
it's killer till the end
when he finds that all I
ever wanted
was to play pretend

no poise, just poison

don't look now
spider's coming
spider's coming
eat your heart out
the spider's coming
to eat your heart out

not too big
but not too small
big enough
to kill us all

poisonous
i'm taken aback,
the only one it should
it turns away from
it turned away from me
and i followed it

peering into the horizon
grey clouds make it hard to see
and its quick body
makes me think
hallucinating

is any of this real
spider closing in
all that matters
falls to the ground
and i am left to bury them

burying emotion
what's the cause of poison

i wish
i wish i was poisoned

clarity

scratched eyes
stumble across dislocated images
scrawled into skin, deep

deep

in dreams

when breathing is slow and
reactions jump as colors fold
fetal in clarity and discolored spirits, praying

praying

over a broken heart

scabbed in bloodied memories
as the continuation of doubt runs
with the moving shadows on the wall, pleading

pleading

to angels and serpents

gathered at the foot of the bed
watching as the last beat, the last breath
shocks the eyes to open blindly

this is how i see you

fingers, carrots, and demerits

a killer and a stew
didn't i always tell you?
denial redial
the phone is missing again
but maybe that's just my heartbeat
to say the least

a killer and a stew
i'll keep watching over you
even with the ball and chain
pain throughout
let's refrain

a killer and a stew
back in 1992
fall back don't relax
a glimpse then
deadweight
body heart mind
limp

a killer and a stew
wash away and undo
life's overdue
smoke away
shoot up
nervous twitches
or addicted missions

a killer and a stew
how about we change the two
maybe lemonade and a thriller too
one too many
steal a ride
two too many

stop the lie
let's make it bloody
i'll make it true
it was never red dye

a killer and a stew
didn't i always tell you?
awkward backyard (charge a dime)
and afterward
let me tell you the truth
it was me and never you

taste of medication in the mourning

receiving common sense
just throw it away
trash it go smash it
just throw it away

it's toxic terror
look in the mirror
look what you see
offer up gold and silver
unless you wish to suffer
surrender to
all the contaminated "carefuls"
what you missed
error by error
smoke more
drink more
stick a needle in my arm
ring the alarm
it's a fierce fire
it's a disastrous desire

receiving common sense
just throw it away
trash it go smash it
just throw it away

it's a contagious colour
conquered by blacks and blues
another midnight horror
watch a movie let it go
let go of physical images
try on this new look, get a new image
imagine
metaphysics
conquer the wolf inside me
breeding demons

needing heathens
to listen to save me save me
from what everyone tells me

receiving common sense
just throw it away
trash it go smash it
just throw it away

conjure up my prince
give me hints
i know i'm a demonstration
of mental aberration
a little bit of confusion
used and useless
mindless self-discussion
allusion to the unknown universe
cantankerous cowards ask about
all the things that no one needs to know
i'll never show
my scars
love's beauty marks

receiving common sense
just throw it away
trash it go smash it
just throw it away

remember the yesterday's goals
we all threw away
what does it matter
if we all fall
we all fall down
explosions from tanks and cannons
recover
admissions i was supposed to say
before this all went astray
car crash call Caroline Ashe
it's a collision and i'm in the middle

i'm stuck in the middle
so i retire my right to burn
i'll return to my mental convulsions
my passions have gone to hell but
at least i still have my poison

receiving common sense
just throw it away
trash it go smash it
just throw it away

i still have my poison
i'm in such an awkward position
i wish i wasn't in
such a deviating delusion as this one
but this is an emergency
call call call hang up hang up
stop pushing my buttons
dial tone died the TV is fried
and all that's left
are superstitions
and apparitions
manifestations
of me

submachine dirty pop

white Bic white hot tip
held against skin melting
blue flame red fingers
shaking

soiled feet buried 2 yards deep
measured twice in skin and bones
in the dark when stars were the first
to go

monumental shift as the mind drifts
between plots and gates heaven and saints
the end is always the future as the future is always
the end

the end…she is…

and the body aches, the body becomes, a vessel
for torture plenty, rips and tears, claws and fears,
feeling

feeling the absent hand, the wondering soul,
closing in, closing

three years, circular conflict, circular grief, circular
searching for
gravity

inspiration was only a thought of you away

the world kept spinning.
not because i kept winning,
but because i could still

laugh, cry, and wonder why;
breathing wasn't sickening
anymore, but freeing

i didn't choke on
my words, because i learned to
be heard. and now there

are still tongue-tied days
but i can articulate
what i need to voice.

there is incessant
noise but i have the power
to overcome it.

i don't need to shout
after every event that
has the power to

destroy me, because
i can let it out just by
letting you know what

i think and the things
i dream: billions of seconds
after this moment.

from you, i have learned.
because of you, i have felt,
and realized the world

keeps spinning today...
not because i keep winning
but because i still

try

the last nail

in silence
wind rustles through branches bare
as leaves are
decomposing in earth

blood moon appearing against imperial clouds
cascading down upon shadows
mourning the last great eclipse
of a soul storming

the ghost of April
haunting October shrill

in a stained glass window
the reflection shattered
of an edge so close yet
still too far away

the cross never felt heavier
around the neck

a broken pew
accepts weight with a groan
as a dusty bible
torments the hands

from behind
an Angel spreads its wings in forgiveness

as the scars are ripping open
and the clotting doesn't start
until it coagulates on the floor
a mixture of oxygen and dreams
heaven is always closer
when you are on your knees

with hands clasped and the head bowed
Jesus appears and puts Band-Aids on the wounds
knowing that strength must come until
March when the last nail in the coffin

can be put in

sub pop machine

electric
vein to machine
tubes and vessels
knot
upon twisting- tongue tied

flash
lights strobe move / ment
blind against
walls and crypts
ghost and scripts
grave watching
shift

blown
tears and wishes
the last eyelash
butterflies and
pale moons
stars in rotation
as a black hole
is seeping
whole

cross
tarnished nails
pulling
splinters from soiled breath
tortured under whiskey
memories
and roses
thorn

sub pop cracks
when the trigger
itches against

callused fingers
and a blood soaked
heart
barely
...
beating

grief

shattered corpse
shelled in skin and scars

shattered corpse
shelled in fiberglass and cloth

shattered corpse made whole
shelled in purple memories

a boy, father, once blue eyed sky
teeters on blurring contacts and bifocals
surrenders to whiskey and mouth full of Prozac

the parasite of greed, want, need, regret,
bleeds the heart onto the sleeve
the parasite of belief, falters knees stained
in remorse and earth still moist from morning's dew

the parasite of grief, builds temples in emotional wastelands

a cigarette burns in an ashtray
outside on a covered entrance
a non-smoking building full of nervous mentalities

chairs are lined symmetrical
in rows of 12
the family
gets the front row
so their tears only wash over their feet

10 yards away
30 fucking feet
360 inches
as the lid closes

under God / Into the Dark

and it's getting harder to
breathe

as hands
stretch
peeled skin
and memories regret
scars and
blood seeping
my body is
wet
as the shower steams
remorse

i lay
silent
against porcelain covered steel
letting every thought
and every moment
slowly slip out of
view
i close my eyes
as i reach out
into the dark
of missing

it's getting harder to breathe

and i've realized
lately
that what you hold you take
and what you've had
you lose
and i've realized
lately
that i know, know

that i will never
see
her
again

and i
am
forgetful of those
reaching out
as my mind doesn't
react
and my words somehow
get lost
and i am in real trouble
real trouble
for i don't mean
as
much
and i can't
replace
and i can't
find the strength
and i am

heading home

under God
the water turns
my body cold
as the heat
of the barrel
rest just under
my chin

and i let go

state of balance

Virgo smiles and darkened eyes
punch drunk against spring solstice
a stagger of breath
ripped skin and
tagged ears

in the medication
alcohol combined
swims thoughts contaminated
with doctors and their high scopes
of pin pointed lasers and of
scalpels of retribution
it's all surgical

five years plus twenty 1 days ago

life was put on hold
holding
hold on

back then, the refurbished
allocation of a dream
of once we had this dream
before time stood still
and the wind changed course
from west to north
there was love
carried forth
in between exhaled Camels
polluting and
suicidal thoughts on the wrong side
of midnight

skin drips
as flesh melts between fingers lost
in the sound of forever

the state of balance
as blue is shelved and
karma is a stray somewhere
in the milky white standby
of nevermore
always wanting, but never needing

crossfire

three days, four nights
and the alcohol swells
in constricted veins

the ashtray smolders
full of exhaled dreams

a small brain bleed
and I'm on my knees
slurring praise to a God
that I could never again believe in

my palms are black
and I've ripped
my nails from my finger tips
digging

April is approaching
and I've reserved
the plot next to hers

four days and I wake
without grace
sipping last night's Jack
as the back wash fills my throat

I scourer the ashtray
for a half smoked Camel
as my fingers
flip back the Japanese lighter
and set my lungs on fire

the Ouija is packed away
or I would be having a one on one
with Lucifer

bringing the dead back to life
as my soul is half eaten
and faith is
a dream that I have expended

mid-day migraine
has pianos playing
in my mind
as I try to remember
the sound of her voice
the touch of her skin
the feel of her laughter
filling the air

Jim has replaced Jack
as I'm on my last fifth
before a weary drive
with bloodshot eyes
and blood stained hands
nicotine and tic tacs on my breath

April is approaching
year five and my friends
say I am spiraling
into this war
as I have withdrawn further
and these bottles
laying on the beige carpet
stained with life and tears
relinquish the hope of a father
for his daughter

May cannot come fast enough
then I will be able to breathe
and these new scars
can start their healing
but until then
Jim and Jack will continue their drowning

and I
will continue to succumb
to faithless pleading

bringing the dead back to life

18

we are the new breed.
with x's over our hearts,
stars with initials scribed into our arms.
we are the promise taken,
the promise fulfilled.
we are the new spies.
the past and the future,
but always the present.
we are silent, but our screams
echo and reverberate.
we have lost faith,
but never the dream.
we are... one

transcontinental sensitivity
sending shivers through
the bones falling in heaps.
sockets of peering eyes move
back and forth back and, still
still, and she gains momentum
finding strength in ash, blowing
into the wind, seven.

it's the love that remains, the love,
she writes in air, thinner, as
hyperventilation controls cursive
finger tips, delicate and pure, polished
in, but the words evaporate when,
the sun dissipates the moisture in breath.

folded upon, folded with, but she never,
as she moves through graves, in and out,
visions perception, loves belief, the greater
of two, the lesser on knees, begging for flight,
for moments to, rewind, re...

and into the clouds sight, sunshine
might, following the wind to, the edge
of sanity. hands, hold out, hold on, turn
cold as the night sweeps away, and the stars
light dims in pulsations, weakening.

the possession

preceding the cars one by
turning slow wheels under
flags ripple in the breeze across

the line
gathers steam sternly
when the sirens wail against
and the flashes of light
beam red

never once wanted to be centered
attentively

shown moon in bright daylight
fascination of the fixation
on

but the morning mourns you

689 divisible

in depth i could remove
the scars that my son just noticed
matching arm for arm
i could
but my sleeves are too short
and my soul is too bare

never witnessed panic

in stress panic becomes a normal progression
into the exception
that is life

and i contemplate
forgiveness with sanity filled

snake eyes
rolling
but
i would rather sit by the grave
and patiently wait
for dusk and the shadows
to follow your every move

purity falters
in callused hands i
try to clean away
regret and trembling
as i search for the proper way
to find a God in my ever deepening
disbelief

in perfect isolation
everything becomes normal

in possession
the fourteen seconds of
your voice replays
even when the volume has been
even as you have been

silenced

the incident

color the sky
in black, no moon, no stars
just, black.

woke from a dreary slumber
noose in shadows, broken windows
and the ability to move
taken.
still focused, with the darken room tainted
light.
closed eyes, wiped, with shaking hands, reopened

light, blurry figure... movement

against the wall, moving, closer
slow torture
slow.

the last breath, the last goodbye
in secret

transcontinental

often in moments i, succumb to
but plagued in, the want beyond the need
and i fall, emotional, standing in foremost
i am captive
held.
always in the promises, always hiding the knife.
stuck in the back
slivered just deep enough.
mindful of the striations on the fourth and fifth rib
pulling slowly
just slow enough that the wound binds
gaping / / / flow.

as the false prophet rust
words of mirrors and a soul embattled.
i tire of the book
words upon words falling, short of forgiveness.

a stain

unremarkable, a test of faith she calls out my name
and memory hands fail to understand the longing.
locked in cold, locked in.
and when i reach out, when i reach
point of breaking, somber.
grief takes the motive and quiet rooms swell.
in screams i watch over and over
as crumbling hearts break
timeless.

it is something we don't talk about

full dark, no stars, no light.
as covers are throat high.
and the cigarette smokes slow
in the ashtray.
the slow flutter.
eyes once again willing to sleep
but dreams, the tumorous dreams
always escape into visions
of blue rooms and breathing tubes
of hands holding on.
hands bringing warmth to the dearest child.
of hands holding on when the heart
fails to comprehend.
forever.

untitled

separate / almost could, count on hands
the stars fell, in dreams / but always indecent
stripped and vulnerable, looked after / after
half and never / whole

urgency in tone / emerging, slow in broken
speak, as lips purge / volumes of regret
in a sea of, but this is home / never
once did protection come / alone

and the flowers, all the pretty flowers / browned
crimson roses stand / with their thorns, still
allowing / fingers and hands to run, over
scarring flesh in two / remorse

the back and forth / grave in mistake, gave
willing my hand / cold, searching for warmth
she / always a pedestal, in search / loved
cascading waterfalls of, love / daughter

rising son

with a match and a little gasoline…

hate bleeds
hands trembling
with scars and Saint Christopher
swinging

a noose around the neck

the ground is frozen
step by step footprints
covered in snow
creeping slow

there. is. an. end. to. this.

ashes to ashes
joining love and memory

the moon looks beyond
full as shadows follow
the curve of the earth
the grit of teeth

closer to the edge

it will start slow
around the foundation
then the heat will build
burning down the house that hate built

the strike of the match…

she meant more than your silent apology.

daisies

nobody could have explained that before i woke

lights, semi-hesitation, tubes and machines, regulating /
steady hands trained in the art of curing,
this was the last procedure they spoke,
the day before was the last day in, as,
you were advised, Saturday love, will be the start of,
going home... Saturday Love... but breathing has
slowed, and the heart has
pushed its' last beat, but the dream continued
'till, the phone rang and distance became
normal.

never watched, ever end...

color the world, purple, with a star bled into the arm
and fingers reminded as two stars combine.
Dearest Jordan, know that i am, be still for tomorrow will,
and my racing heart has learned new ways to combine,
but faith in plans and sacrifice falter when,
Jesus, he speaks in small whispers, i try to drown out,
washing away in tantrums of alcohol and regret.

faith.

thirty minutes, the pressure on your chest, the lightness of,
breath. and i stare over and over at the charts and notes, running
my fingers over your heartbeat on paper, till, the line falls flat,
in my ever diseased mind, the alarms and codes fill my ears,
tears fill and my hands shake. i never saw you go, never said,
Love.

i used to count the days, then weeks, months,
a reversal of a newborn.
19 months, 5 days.

my mother has said, losing you has made me more, human.
i am just overwhelmed, i have tried to explain to her, the art of
balance / suffering / life / and the everyday knowledge that
hits me in the chest, that you are never coming back, that
as human as i may seem, all of this is just a façade of suffering.

blocking out the world, with headphones on and music streaming,
i have put Blue on the shelf, in the attempt to close a chapter
that constantly pulls me back in, another hook, another verse,
another night where sleep is the cousin of death and i, force my
eyes wide. force my heart to beat, just, beat.

Saturday Love, as i held your hand for the last…

it is all i think about.

conversation

it is a funny thing, keeping safe, pushing
away, locking trap doors, in haste
emotional distance, she stays
close

i keep believing
in the conversation, even as, my voice
remains, alone, but, i know, know
nothing as much, as
that sinking feeling tomorrow will
be, but she is and i

if Jesus was here, right next, tolerance would
end, and battling the demons, i could should succumb
but my fist are already bloodied
and there isn't will enough to
control, numb

lights, action… you might want a picture
before
the whiskey takes hold and i become
another

closer she remains, and her mother just confuses
maybe it is just the species
or my forever ledge soul in the grip of
tendencies known only, inward

but the conversation still, continues
alone

blinding

she says, "let me tell you of forgiveness,
of the morning with light, waking,
with the weight taken off your shoulders,
and a heart that can beat,
without the infinite grief pounding,"
she says…

in the backroom
visions of ash lined hallways
and tumbling clocks ticking
away
slowly stumbling from bottle to the next
the bed calls
a lonesome idea of gone
enters into the broken process
of thinking that tomorrow is…

and with might
solitude formal, scrubbing away
the black suit is pressed but
stained
as weary eyes slumber without
while tears focus on
the everyday blinding
binding

closer, closer, closer it becomes
the air swirls cold
with the sleet and the snow mixing
April has passed
and the leaves are browned with decay
just as
saving borrows the Jesus piece and
falls to soiled knees begging

all along the combining union

seeks closing eyes
while pain is managed
by never looking into the mirror
knowing age has taken
the faltering heart and broken
the spirit

another cigarette has lost its nicotine draw
while the whiskey burns down the throat

holding on with both hands
tied to the dream
in the middle of the night
a familiar voice wakes
to a scream
knowing that losing her was
the end of the best part
of living

more mechanical
than human, as touch becomes
a secret that withholds
the warmth of a daughter saying
goodbye
in an isolated blue room with
the walls bare
and the quiet heart
battered, showing its bruises,
turning purple

the violence of regret
tremors down abstaining
silhouettes of understanding
failing to control
the never ending rabbit hole
that consumes every waking
memory

alas, the dream now is

the plot next to,
with a shade of bronze
and the words of a father
to his daughter
resting eternal

she says, "let me tell you of forgiveness…"

atmospheres

in depth, Wrenching, tongue tied and
failing to scream A shortness of
ease, a breath relaxing Breathe
the closet lined, migraine pills,
milligrams of, secondary Emotion
create, Sensory commotion- release

maybe in the rays, Sunshine death, believe
a miracle of hyper religious tendencies
with faulty knees Forged hands and a
Rusted cross, still, a child's wake Ever
listening, in the dark Wanting

in dirt bronze and Marble hold, frozen
flowers Grave, giving tears, anomalies
in perspective, Remember when, yesterday
was then Precious, a voice carried Verse
and choice, Rhyme and function
brought Form to, reaching soul to Soul

but, silence has Silenced even when
the rain flows Rivers down, the Throat
stand by, Forever, the petals, hope
Jars, atmospheres disruption, falling
heart to Heart hand to, empty

touch

April

the soft freeze, pillowing against the gusting exhale
spring is tormenting, March snowflakes against the grave
under the full moon pass and shortened quakes

I say her name

again in silence, the mistakes flower and grow
in a troubled speaking mind, yesterday plows
away the smile that faded when April rained

I say her name

overthrown, losing faith I pretend, in the days
leading, that Angels flew into that blue room
and removed the pain that swept over

I say her name

bruised, scarred hands bend, wiping away
tears that form ice, this heart, broken down
begging for just one more touch

I say her name…

blending

assemble
as whiskey washes
away

the slow tourniquet blending soul to
skin bending time space continuance

quiet room swells blue

hand to hand

first born remains

pillows in ash subtle dreams stir

religious markers on chest screaming

Saint Christopher marches
to a broken heart beaten into
submission
protecting
the full star around the neck
pastfuturepresent

distortion

occupational membrane
a spider stuck in
the tub
with its eight legs
tap tap tapping
on ruptured glass

amusing disguise
closely watched
radiation forced through
closed eyes visioning
ghost- she comes
as dreams slow to fog
and the colors, the colors
run out of breath
hands to chest

tied to a string
with a pull and a tug
the heart begins to
believe shadows dancing
on midnights lying
tongue
everything becomes
an attrition of skin
bleeding in
veins tattooed with
stars lining

as the doctor with his
sour voice beckons the
wake
as black dresses eyes
barely fluttering after
the white light reaches
deep in sockets

electrifying the smoke
billowing from punctured
lungs begging as the first strike
of this war
led to the death of the daughter
so pure
so loved
so wanted

but the spider
the goddamn spider
with its fucking legs
tapping
stirs the soul
enables a fear
creating nightmares
of never coming home

never

coming

home

and in this state
state of distortion raging
ragged
grasping for any
miracle
that could bring back
bring back
the dear lost loved
daughter

i am
crushed

the long road

i remember
the last time i held you

i remember before
burial plots of brown
the rain of April coming down
and hair curled that was never curly

i remember before
the quiet of the blue room
removal of the breathing tube
and the somberness of our last conversation

i remember before
trips to the "IMA"
the Sunbird that broke down at the steak house
and "The Men Who Stare at Goats"

i remember before
my scars set in motion
the alcohol blubbering
one star into two on the phone

i remember before
our home before the alien crash landed
putt putt championships
and smiles overflowing

i remember before
your scars took over
medication became your soldier
and music was your best friend

i remember before
the muffler sparked the ground

the move down south
and how Code Red came through your nose

i remember before
blue lights and Nerf dart fights
the big screen TV and you slumbering on the couch
fishing trips with fake bait and you never learning how to cast

i remember before
your words found a home on paper
the rhyming game between equal foes
Starbucks and late night scary movies

i remember before
the small house with a yard
your hair cut way too short
and Pearly getting lost

i remember before
the sand in your shoes from the park
how high on the swings was never high enough
your first bike with wide black wheels

i remember before
pumpkins that were never big enough
Halloweens with too much makeup
and when dresses were something you loved

i remember before
the first snowflake touched your nose
how bundled up you were in your pink coat
how blue your eyes were before they turned hazel

i remember before
the small apartment on Rogers
the green carpet and you throwing things in the toilet
and how small you were in your crib

i remember before

your first Purdue onesie
the extremely stinky diaper
and your gorgeous smile

i remember
the first time i held you

I would like to personally thank Tony Avellana for the formatting help, Elaine Ward for the cover design and being patient with all the small edits I asked for, Danielle and Chris for the layout help, Betty and Ivy for cover and formatting work on two previous books.

I would also like to thank Jeff for being more than family to me, you've kept my thoughts focused on the next day instead of the past. Mel, your grace and understanding has kept me safe; you allow me to vent, to cry, to laugh, and to release all of my world without any hesitation. Tara, thank you for just being you, you do deserve that unicorn. Amanda (Poodles), pancakes will never be the same.

Drew, you are the rock that holds me in place, I love you boy.

Catherine, although our words no longer find a home with each other, we created two wonderful children, and your strength and patience allowed me to grow as a man and a father.

Jordan, I could write about you for the rest of my life, we shared a bond that, even in your death, cannot be broken. You are the inspiration for me to be a better parent to Drew, a better human being, and a better writer.

I love you, I miss you…

www.ingramcontent.com/pod-product-compliance
Lightning Source LLC
LaVergne TN
LVHW011210080426
835508LV00007B/714